OX[
1000

He Cannot Really Read

by Mary Cockett

pictures by Prudence Seward

OXFORD UNIVERSITY PRESS

Oxford University Press, Walton Street, Oxford OX2 6DP

OXFORD NEW YORK TORONTO
DELHI BOMBAY CALCUTTA MADRAS KARACHI
PETALING JAYA SINGAPORE HONG KONG TOKYO
NAIROBI DAR ES SALAAM CAPE TOWN
MELBOURNE AUCKLAND

and associated companies in
BERLIN IBADAN

OXFORD and OXFORD ENGLISH
are trade marks of Oxford University Press

ISBN 0 19 421784 1

© *Oxford University Press, 1975*

First published 1975
Seventh impression 1990

Printed in Hong Kong

1 A holiday

The children were leaving the classroom. They were laughing and talking. It was the beginning of a short holiday.

One of the boys said to the teacher, 'I'm going to stay with my grandfather, Miss Mandy.'

One of the girls said, 'We're going to stay on a farm.'

Miss Mandy thought, 'Most of the children aren't going to go anywhere.' Then she said, 'Have a good time, everybody, and look after your books. Goodbye, all of you.'

'Goodbye, Miss Mandy.'

Matthew was still in the classroom. He was reading. He was waiting for John Adams.

Miss Mandy said, 'That's a long book, Matthew.'

'Yes,' said Matthew. 'It's got a hundred and twenty-eight pages.'

'But you read really well now, don't you?'

They smiled at each other.

John heard Miss Mandy and Matthew talking. He was still trying to choose a book. He thought, 'Matthew doesn't throw balls straight, but I do. Matthew doesn't run fast or jump high, but I do. But Matthew reads well, and I don't. I want to read. I'm going to read really well.'

Miss Mandy said, 'Are you ready, John? What have you got? Oh, yes, a book about cars and trains. It's got good pictures, hasn't it?' She looked at his sad face. 'What are you going to do in the holiday, John?'

'Oh, I'm going to play football and try to read my book and I'll go to Matthew's house. I'll play with Elizabeth too.'

'Who looks after her while your father's at the factory?'

'Mrs Scott. She lives in the next house. Elizabeth likes her.'

'Are you going to visit your mother at the hospital?'

'No, Miss Mandy. They don't let children go. My father goes every evening.'

'Who cooks for you?'

'I sometimes do. I cooked breakfast for my father last week.'

'Good!' said Miss Mandy. She smiled, and then John smiled too. 'Well, help your father and play football, but don't forget to read every day.'

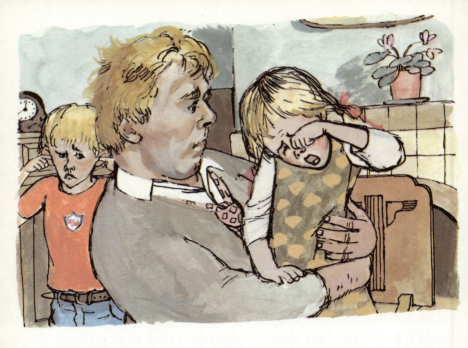

2 At home

That evening John's sister Elizabeth cried because her mother was not there. Her father tried to make her feel better. He talked to her and carried her to bed. 'Don't cry, Elizabeth. Mother will be better soon, and then she'll come home again.'

But Elizabeth cried and said, 'But I want my Mum now! I want her now!'

The noise was terrible. John put his fingers in his ears. At last Elizabeth went to sleep.

John turned the radio on and listened to some music. He began to play marbles. Suddenly Mr Adams turned the radio off.

'Stop playing marbles,' he said angrily. 'Find something useful to do.'

'What? What do you want me to do?'

'Get your school book.'

John opened the book, but after a minute he came to a difficult word. He looked up and said, 'What's this word, please, Dad?'

'Don't ask me,' said Mr Adams. 'I've had a hard day, and I'm very tired.' He looked tired too, and soon he was asleep in his chair.

John looked out of the window. He wanted to go out and play with his friends, but instead he sat down and looked at his book again. He read some of the words under the bright pictures.

As soon as his father opened his eyes, John said, 'You've had a good sleep, haven't you?'

'Not really,' said Mr Adams. 'I'm still tired.' He looked at John's book. 'Oh, that's a nice picture. I've travelled on an old train like that one.' John asked him about another word, but his father said, 'The light isn't strong enough, and it's late now. Put your book away and go to bed.' He did not speak angrily. He looked sad. In a few minutes he was asleep again.

Quietly John went to bed. He was sad too. His mother always smiled at him and said, 'Good night. Sleep well.'

On Saturday morning John played football with his friends. When he got home he said to his father, 'I wanted Matthew to help me with my book, but he's out. Will you help me?'

'I've got too much work to do,' his father answered. 'Miss Mandy's your teacher, isn't she? It's important for you to learn, but I'm very busy. I'm going to paint the walls and the ceiling of the living-room.'

'Oh, are you? Mum *will* be surprised.'

'Yes. She'll be pleased. Those walls need painting. They'll look nice when she comes home.'

'What colour will you paint them?'

'What colour do you think?'

'Yellow,' said John, 'but not bright yellow.'

'You're right,' said his father. 'Will you help me to wash the walls? And then we'll buy the paint.'

'Oh, yes,' John said happily.

They borrowed a ladder from Mrs Scott. They moved the furniture into the middle of the room. Together they washed the walls, and then they went out and bought some yellow paint.

John watched his father painting. Mr Adams
talked to him about painting with a big brush.

'You're good at it,' said John. 'You're quick
too.'

'Painting a wall isn't difficult,' his father said.
'I'm beginning to be hungry, aren't you?'

'Yes, I am,' said John. 'Let me make the lunch.'

He went into the kitchen. He wanted to cook something different. There was a tin of food on the shelf. John looked at it, but the words on the tin were difficult to read. He took it into the living-room. His father was on the ladder.

'What are these words, Dad?' John asked.

'Oh, I don't know,' said his father. 'I can't see the words from here. Perhaps I need glasses.'

So John cooked eggs and potatoes. That was easy. He and his father had a picnic in the sun outside the kitchen door. They were away from the smell of paint there.

3 The tap

After their meal Mr Adams said, 'Listen to that tap, John. Turn it off, please.'

'I tried, but it doesn't stop. I'll try again.'

It was useless. The water still got through. *Drip. Drop. Drip drop drip. Drip. Drip drop. Drip drip drip drop.*

'That tap!' said Mr Adams. 'It needs a new washer, John. Run to the shop, and buy me one.'

'A washer?'

'Ask for a washer for a cold tap.'

'But where? Which shop?'

'The shop by the cinema. We bought the paint there. Here's some money. Oh, it's started to rain. Put your coat on, but hurry up. That tap! I'm going to turn the water off. It's really running now.'

John ran too. He enjoyed running in the rain. He bought the washer without any trouble. It was hard and flat and round, and it had a hole in the middle. 'How does a washer stop a tap dripping?' he thought.

When he got home again, John watched his father take the top off the tap. Then Mr Adams

took the old washer out. 'There! Look at that!' It
was thin and broken. He put the new washer in.
Soon the tap was ready.

'That's clever,' said John.

His father was pleased, but he only said, 'When
you know the right way, it's easy.'

'It's clever, I think.'

That evening John showed his school book to
his little sister.

'Look, Elizabeth, this is an old train. Look at
the thick smoke.'

He made the noise of the old train, and Elizabeth made the noise of the old train too.

Then John said, 'This next train works by electricity. It doesn't make any smoke.'

Elizabeth did not understand, but she thought, 'John's clever.' Then Elizabeth told John the colours of some of the cars in the book, and he said, 'You're a clever girl.'

Mr Adams smiled at John. 'That was kind of you,' he said.

A few days later Mrs Scott brought her radio and said to Mr Adams, 'Will you help me with this, please, Mr Adams. My husband tried to mend it, but it's still broken. He never mends things well.'

Mr Adams said, 'But he grows beautiful plants, and I've never learnt to do that.'

'When my husband mends things, they always break again,' Mrs Scott said. 'Oh, you've painted the living-room. Those walls *are* a pretty colour! Your wife *will* be pleased.'

It was difficult to mend the radio, and it took a long time, but Mr Adams did it. Mrs Scott never stopped talking, but she cooked a big meal for everybody. Elizabeth went to sleep at the table, and her father carried her to bed. She did not cry that night.

For the first time John thought about all his father's good work in their house. When he mended things, they did not break.

Every day the next week John played football. Most of the boys were older than John, but he was good at football, so they let him play. Every day John read to Matthew, and every day he read a little better.

4 The letter

At school two weeks later Miss Mandy said to the class, 'We're all going to go to the seaside for the day next Monday.'

'Hooray!' somebody shouted.

'Wait! I haven't finished. This afternoon I'm going to give each child a letter and a card to take home. Listen. The letter says:

"Next Monday we are going to study sand and

rocks and animals at the seaside. We will get some cheap tickets for the train journey. The school will pay for the tickets, but each child will need to bring food for two meals. We are going to leave school at 9 a.m. Please be punctual. We will not get back to school until 7 p.m. Keep this letter, but please write, 'Yes' or 'No' on the card. Put your child's name on it, and let me have it tomorrow."'

Then Miss Mandy said, 'Remember to bring the card tomorrow, or you won't go to the seaside. But ask your parents nicely.'

John nearly forgot about the letter. He played football that evening. Then he listened to the radio. He was going to bed when he remembered the letter in his pocket.

He showed it to his father. Mr Adams was angry. He opened the letter, but he did not read it. He put it behind the clock.

'Oh,' said John, 'aren't you going to read it?'

'No. Your mother likes seeing letters from school. I'll take it to her tomorrow.'

'Yes, take it tomorrow, then,' said John, 'but please write "Yes" and my name on the card.'

'I'm hot and tired,' said Mr Adams, 'and I'm trying to iron my shirt. I'm too busy to read that letter. What does your teacher want?'

John told his father about the day at the sea.
'The school will pay for the tickets, and Miss
Mandy will buy them tomorrow. Please let me go.
Please write "Yes" and my name on the card.'

So Mr Adams did. He wrote very slowly. John
thought, 'He's slow at writing because he's tired
and he's angry with me.' He said, 'Thank you
very much, Dad. Good night.'

'Good night, John.'

5 Another letter

The next day Mr Adams found a piece of paper under the door. He picked it up, but instead of reading it, he put it in his pocket.

'Who's that for? Who put it there?' asked John.

But Mr Adams did not answer. 'I'm in a hurry,' he said. 'It's nearly time for the hospital. I'm going to go by bus.' He washed his hands and face and drank some tea. Then he went out of the house.

A few minutes later Mrs Scott came to the door with some beautiful, red roses.

'These are for your mother, John,' she said. 'Your father hasn't gone, has he?'

'Yes, he's gone to the bus. I'm sorry, Mrs Scott.'

Then John remembered the piece of paper. 'Oh,' he said, 'did you put a letter about the roses under the door?'

'Yes, I did,' said Mrs Scott.

'I'll give them to him,' said John. 'I'll catch him.'

'It's too far!'

'No it isn't!' John took the roses and thanked
her. He began running to the bus-stop. He ran
like the wind. He thought, 'Will I get to the
bus-stop before the bus? Oh, why did Dad go
without the flowers?'

As soon as John got to the bus-stop, the bus
came round the corner. He pushed the roses into
his father's hand. 'These are from Mrs Scott.
Why did you go without them? Why didn't you
read her letter?'

'I forgot,' said Mr Adams, but his face looked
strange. 'I'm very sorry. Oh, I've forgotten to
bring your school letter.'

He got on to the bus and waved to John. The bus moved away, but John stood thinking. 'I know something about my father, but he doesn't want me to know it,' he thought. 'He does a lot of things well. He does his work at the factory well. He paints walls well. He puts washers on taps. He mends radios. He does much more than a lot of other fathers, but he can't really read.

'When I wanted him to help me with words, he always had an excuse. He was tired, or it was late and the light wasn't strong enough, or he was painting, or the words were too small. Then he was ironing. He can't really read! But he didn't want me to know.'

John felt cold. He held on to the bus-stop very hard.

6 Learning together

Much later Matthew found John still standing there.

'Where are you going, John?' he asked.

John looked at him. 'I'm not going anywhere,' he said.

'What are you doing here, then?'

'Nothing.'

'Come and play,' said Matthew.

'All right,' John said. 'Do you want to play marbles?'

'You always win,' said Matthew, but he walked home with John.

When they got home, John took the school letter from behind the clock.

'Will you read this to me first, Matthew?' he asked. 'You read really well.'

Matthew read all the words, the short ones and the long ones, the easy ones and the difficult ones, without any trouble.

John said, 'Oh, it isn't very difficult. I didn't try very hard. Where's the word "journey"?'

'There. That's "journey".'

'And Miss Mandy wants us to bring food for *two* meals. I didn't hear her say that.'

Matthew cleaned his glasses. 'Didn't your father tell you?' he asked.

'No,' said John. 'He forgot.' That was not true, and it was not kind, he thought. His father was good at remembering. When you cannot read, you listen hard and you try to remember. But John did not want to tell Matthew about his father.

Matthew read the letter again slowly. Then John tried, and Matthew helped him with some of the words. It was not really difficult. Then they played marbles behind the house. Matthew won nearly every game!

'You're not very good tonight, are you, John?' he said.

John only said, 'I don't always win.'

Matthew went home with a bag full of marbles. He was very pleased.

When Mr Adams came home, he said, 'Your mother's *much* better, John.'

'Oh, good! When's she going to come home?'

'Oh, I don't know the answer to that,' he said, but as he cleaned his shoes, he looked very happy.

John said, 'Matthew helped me to read the school letter. Do you want me to read it to you while you're cleaning your shoes?'

'Yes, please.'

So John read it all.

'You read that very well,' his father said. 'What's that word?'

'It's "tomorrow",' John said.

'That's right,' said Mr Adams. He pointed to other words, and John read those too. It was like playing a game. John was teaching his father, but he did not let his father know. They both worked hard reading the letter.

Then Mr Adams said, 'I told your mother about the day at the sea, but I'll remember to take the letter tomorrow. Now I'm hungry. Are you?'

'Yes,' said John. 'Let's have some food.'

While they were eating cheese sandwiches, Mr Adams said, 'When people can't read easily, lots of words look difficult. I didn't like school, and I've forgotten lots of words. Your mother's quite good at reading.'

John said nothing. He thought, 'I don't want him to say, "I can't really read".' Then he remembered something: his mother always read the school letters. Sometimes she wrote letters too, but his father never wrote any.

The next day Mr Adams said, 'I've got some good news.'

'What? Is Mum going to come home soon?'

'Yes, in three days' time.'

'Hooray!' John shouted.

'We'll clean the house and we'll make something nice to eat.'

And they did. John made a chocolate cake.
Mr Adams polished the floor and bought some
flowers. When Mrs Adams came home she looked
thin, but her eyes were shining. Elizabeth laughed
and danced all round the room.

One evening a week later Mr Adams got ready to go out.

'Where are you going?' asked John.

Mr Adams did not say anything, but he showed John a piece of paper. John looked at it. He read: 'Reading classes for . . .' John looked at his father.

'What's that word, please?' he asked.

Mr Adams looked at the word. 'Adults,' he said and smiled.

John smiled at his father and gave the piece of paper back to him.

Mum = Mother
Dad = Father

John and Elizabeth say 'Mum' instead of 'Mother'.
John and Elizabeth say 'Dad' instead of 'Father'.

Adult = More than 18 years old
Elizabeth's mother is an adult.
Teachers and policemen are adults too.

Drip
Washer
This is a tap. This is a washer.
The tap is dripping like this:
drip, drip, drip, drop, drip.

Polish
Mr Adams is going to clean
these shoes. Then he is going
to polish them.
The boy's shoes are dirty.
The girl's shoes are dirty.

Mr Adams has cleaned the shoes. Look at them. They are clean.
Now Mr Adams has polished the shoes. Look at them. They are
shining.

Can(not) read

John can see the words, but he is
a long way away. He cannot read them.

Now John is near. He can see the
words and he knows them.
He can read them. He is shouting
the words: 'Dangerous. Do not
bathe here.' So he is not going to
bathe there.

Answer these questions

1 *A holiday*
What does John do well?
What is the name of John's sister?
Where does John's father work?
What is John going to do in the holiday?
Where is his mother?
What did the teacher say to John about reading?

2 *At home*
Why did Mr Adams turn the radio off angrily? What was John
doing?
What did John want to do when his father went to sleep?
Why is Mr Adams going to paint the walls?
John and his father borrowed something from Mrs Scott. What was it?
Where does Mrs Scott live?

3 *The tap*
What did the tap need?
Before Mr Adams took the top off the tap, what did he do?
What did Mrs Scott say about the colour of the walls?
Was it easy for Mr Adams to mend the radio?
While Mr Adams was mending the radio, what was Mrs Scott doing?
Why did the older boys let John play football with them?

4 *The letter*

Who will pay for the train tickets?

Do the children need to take food to the seaside?

Did the teacher want the children to bring their letters and cards to school?

When John took the letter home, what did he do with it?

Mr Adams did not read the school letter. What did he say?

5 *Another letter*

What did Mrs Scott put under the door?

What did Mrs Scott bring to the door?

What did she say to John?

How did Mr Adams go to the hospital?

What happened as soon as John reached the bus-stop?

6 *Learning together*

What did Matthew say when he found John at the bus-stop?

Is Mr Adams good at remembering?

Who usually wins at marbles?

While Mr Adams was cleaning his shoes, what did John do?

Who wrote the letters at John's house?

What did Elizabeth do when her mother came home?

Which of these words are opposites?

1 remember   easy
2 clean   lose
3 difficult   forget
4 win   break
5 mend   dirty

Which of these words mean the same?

1 start   go to see
2 out   watch
3 visit   every
4 look at   not in
5 each   begin

Make a story out of these sentences:

He thought, 'My mother always reads the letters.'

Then Mr Adams went to reading classes.

Mrs Adams came home from the hospital.

Elizabeth cried and cried. She wanted her mother.

John cooked for his father and showed pictures to his sister.

John said to his father, 'Please help me with my school book.'

Mrs Adams was ill and at the hospital.

But his father painted the walls.

John discovered something about his father. 'He does a lot of things well, but he can't really read!'

About you

Do you play any games?

Do you cook?

Have you got a sister?

What time do you get up?

Do you go to school by bus?

What kind of breakfast do you have?

Do you enjoy running in the rain?

How many things do you read each day? Do you read words in shop windows, or on tins of food, or in newspapers?

Take the first letter away from each of these words, and you will find different words. What are they?

smile	wall
clock	hear
train	every
nice	that
farm	mother

What are these?

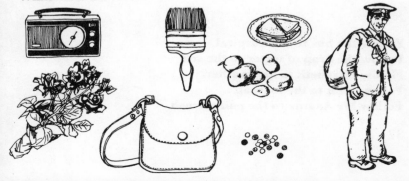

Follow the bus to the hospital.
Follow the drop of water to the sea.
Follow Elizabeth to her mother.
Follow John to the football
Follow Mr Adams to the paint brush.